All About Hawaiian

All About Hawaiian

Albert J. Schütz

A Kolowalu Book

UNIVERSITY OF HAWAI'I PRESS

HONOLULU

98 99 00   2 3 4 5

Library of Congress Cataloging-in-Publication Data

Schütz, Albert J., 1936–
All about Hawaiian/Albert J. Shütz
p.   cm.
"A Kolowalu book."
ISBN 0-8248-1686-2
1. Hawaiian language—Grammar.
2. English language—Dictionaries—Hawaiian.
3. Hawaii—Languages—Vocabulary.   I. Title.
PL 6443.S38   1995
499'.4—dc20
95-1632
CIP

Designed by Paula Newcomb

Contents

All About Hawaiian

Introduction

Whether you are a *kamaʻāina* (child of the land) or a *malihini* (visitor), you undoubtedly take pleasure in those attractions that Hawaiʻi is best known for: its fabled climate, its beaches, and its spectacular scenery. But Hawaiʻi is more than just a collection of geographical features—it has a culture of its own as well. And one way to experience part of this culture is through the Hawaiian language.

Even though Hawaiian is no longer widely spoken, you are still surrounded by the language. If you're arriving at the islands for the first time, or returning home after a holiday, you're greeted with *Aloha!* (hello, welcome), perhaps given a flower *lei* (garland), and led to the *wikiwiki* (quick) bus that takes you to the baggage claim area at the airport. If you're headed to *Waikīkī* (spouting water: it was once a swampy area), driving around the island, or simply heading home, you'll notice that most street and place names are Hawaiian as well.

In order to show respect for the language, it's important to learn how to pronounce Hawaiian words correctly. For example, what's the right way to say *Hawaiʻi*? And by the way, what's that backwards apostrophe in the word? And the line over the *i*'s in *Waikīkī*? Actually, they're not just punctuation marks, but essential parts of the word.

Going back further in time, we're confronted with more puzzles. For example, why did the early explorers write *aloha* as *aroha*? In fact, before 1826, Hawaiian was written with several letters that are no longer used: *b*, *d*, *r*, *t*, and *v*. When these letters were dropped from the alphabet, some people felt that the language had been diminished or demeaned somehow. In this book, you'll see why this is not true.

You'll also see some examples of how Hawaiian and English have borrowed from each other, each enriching its own vocabulary with gifts from the other language.

Although you can't expect to learn how to speak Hawaiian from this one brief description, the grammatical sketch provided here will show you something about the structure of the language, and the word lists will introduce you to the everyday Hawaiian words you're most likely to hear or see.

Further, a look at current efforts to preserve the language will give you some idea of the future of Hawaiian.

All in all, if you try to learn something about Hawaiian —its history, its pronunciation, and its prospects for the future—you will broaden your own horizons, and your stay here, whether for a week or a lifetime, will be enriched.

A Note on the Illustrations

The pictures reproduced here, some of which illustrate a particular part of the language and others merely decorate, are from *O ke Kumumua na na Kamalii; He Palapala e Ao aku ai i na Kamalii Ike Ole i ka Heluhelu Palapala* (First lessons for children; a book teaching those children who do not know how to read books), by John S. Emerson, 1835. As evidence of how widespread reading and writing in Hawaiian were at this time, 52,000 copies of this primer were printed between 1835 and 1844. The woodblock prints, as well as the first page of the 1822 Hawaiian alphabet, are reproduced here through the kind permission of the Hawaiian Mission Children's Society.

Where Does Hawaiian Come From?

Hawaiian belongs to the Polynesian language family, most of which is spread over a large triangular area in the Pacific Ocean, with Hawai'i at the northernmost corner, New Zealand (Aotearoa), where Māori is spoken, to the southwest, and Easter Island (Rapanui) to the southeast. Polynesian is more remotely related to many languages further west—including Fijian, Malagasy, Malay, and the languages of the Philippines.

Within the Polynesian family, some of Hawaiian's closest relatives are Tahitian, Marquesan, and Māori; more distant relatives are Samoan and Tongan. Here, "distant" doesn't refer to geography, but to the time that has passed since these now-separate languages were spoken as a single language in one community.

Barring earlier Spanish contact—an intriguing but as yet unproved possibility—the outside world received its first glimpse of Hawaiian through the published journals of Captain James Cook, who with his crew sighted the island of Kaua'i on 18 January 1778. On hearing the language for the first time, the explorers were immediately struck by its closeness to Tahitian and Māori in spite of the great dis-

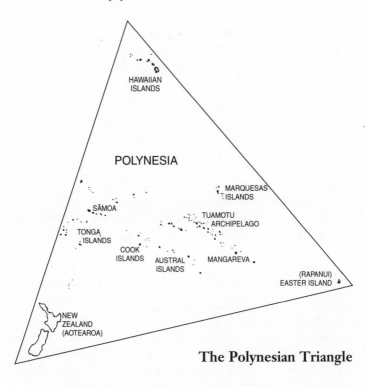

The Polynesian Triangle

tances that separate the island groups. In fact, many early observers thought that Hawaiian and many other Pacific languages were all dialects of one widespread language: Polynesian. This view is easy to understand, for in the late eighteenth century, the various Polynesian languages were much more similar than they are now. (One of the reasons Tahitian has changed so much since then is that a word-taboo system called *pi'i* was in effect there, forcing the language to change words, and even syllables, that were similar to those in the name of a chief who had died.) But the main reason for considering Polynesian one language was that Cook and his crew (who knew some Tahitian from their extended stays in the Society Islands) and the Hawaiians were able to communicate on a fairly elementary level. If they chose very common words, the chances are that the languages seemed almost identical. For example, see how similiar the numbers are in the three Polynesian languages below:

	HAWAIIAN	TAHITIAN	MĀORI
one	*kahi*	*tahi*	*tahi*
two	*lua*	*piti*	*rua*
three	*kolu*	*toru*	*toru*
four	*hā*	*maha*	*whā*
five	*lima*	*pae*	*rima*
six	*ono*	*ono*	*ono*
seven	*hiku*	*hitu*	*whitu*
eight	*walu*	*va'u*	*waru*
nine	*iwa*	*iva*	*iwa*
ten	*'umi*	*ahuru*	*tekau*

It's not just the numbers that are similar. Many other words, especially those used most often, are also the same—or nearly so—in the three languages:

	HAWAIIAN	TAHITIAN	MĀORI
bird	*manu*	*manu*	*manu*
canoe	*wa'a*	*va'a*	*waka*
child	*kamali'i*	*tamari'i*	*tamaiti*

drink	*inu*	*inu*	*inu*
face	*maka*	*mata*	*mata*
fish	*i'a*	*i'a*	*ika*
fly	*lele*	*rere*	*rere*
hand	*lima*	*rima*	*ringa*
head	*po'o*	*ūpo'o*	*ūpoko*
house	*hale*	*fare*	*whare*
moon	*malama*	*marama*	*marama*
night	*pō*	*pō*	*pō*
person	*kanaka*	*ta'ata*	*tangata*
power	*mana*	*mana*	*mana*
rain	*ua*	*ua*	*ua*
sea	*moana*	*moana*	*moana*
sick	*ma'i*	*ma'i*	*maki*
skin	*'ili*	*'iri*	*kiri*
sky	*lani*	*ra'i*	*rangi*
tooth	*niho*	*niho*	*niho*
turtle	*honu*	*honu*	*honu*
what?	*aha*	*aha*	*aha*
woman	*wahine*	*vahine*	*wahine*

For over forty years after first contact, the only records of Hawaiian were the dozen or so word lists collected by explorers or beachcombers, and casual observations written in travel accounts. Serious work on the language began in 1820 with the arrival of the Protestant missionaries from New England, who realized that if they were to succeed in their goal of converting the people to Christianity, the Hawaiians had to be able to read and write their own language.

Spelling and Pronunciation

Early Impressions

One of the first impressions visitors had of the Hawaiian language was that it was simple and childlike. But this was merely their naive perception of a language that was very different from European languages. Besides, according to one observer, the Hawaiians simplified their language when they spoke to outsiders, so that what they heard was not natural Hawaiian, but a type of "foreigner talk."

More flattering—but equally vague—adjectives that have been used to describe what Hawaiian sounds like are "smooth," "soft with a musical sound," "fluid," and "melodious." One nineteenth-century writer even compared the language to the warbling of birds!

Why such characterizations? There are two possible reasons. The first is that, unlike English, Hawaiian has no consonant clusters, and every syllable ends with a vowel. Thus, the ratio of vowels to consonants is relatively high. Second, Hawaiian has no sibilants (*s*-like sounds), a characteristic that endears the language to singers, more so even than Italian.

Creating an Alphabet

He bu-ke.

He i-pu i-ni-ka.

The key to literacy (and hence, conversion), the missionaries believed, was an efficient alphabet and writing system. After several false starts (including a scheme to write two of the vowels with numbers rather than letters), the missionaries decided to write the vowels in the European, rather than the English, fashion. They found five distinct sounds, closely matching those in Latin or Italian, that could be conveniently represented by the five vowel letters available in the Roman alphabet.

Another point in this system's favor was that it was already used by the Tahitian Mission, and before it was known how different the two languages actually were, it was hoped that Hawaiians would be able to read books printed in Tahitian.

Once the European use of the vowel letters was adopted, spellings such as those on the left below (as written by one of Captain Cook's crew) were changed to those on the right:

neeho	tooth	*niho*
eihoo	nose	*ihu*
pahoo	drum	*pahu*

The consonants, however, were another matter, for several of them seemed to vary at random. For example, it made no difference whether a word was pronounced with *k* or *t*: the name of the conquering chief Kamehameha was first written *Tamehameha* (in fact, one early missionary complained that he had seen the name written twelve or fourteen different ways). On Kaua'i and Ni'ihau, *t* seems to have been used exclusively, but we can see that in the early word lists collected on the other islands, observers wrote both letters, sometimes evenly distributed. Other so-called pairs — *v~w* and *l~r* — were more a matter of the sound being neither one nor the other, but instead, something between the two. But the English writing system makes no provision for such sounds. Therefore, most people insisted on writing whichever sound they thought they heard, with the result that any word containing at least one of these problem consonants could be written in different ways—an obvious obstacle to literacy and an insurmountable barrier to compiling a dictionary. The solution to this problem was to choose one letter for each of these groups, a move that made Hawai'i's writing system very efficient—so efficient, in fact, that one missionary wrote in 1827: "With our present alphabet a boy of fourteen, with common intelligence may in one month become a perfect master of the orthography of his language and be able to read and write the whole of it with correctness."

Contrast this with the time it takes to learn to read and write English perfectly!

Still, two sounds remained largely unwritten, since there was no conventional way to indicate them at that time. The

THE ALPHABET.

VOWELS.		SOUND.	
	Names.	*Ex. in Eng.*	*Ex. in Hawaii.*
A a ---â	as in *father*,	la—sun.
E e ---a	— *tete*,	hemo—cast off.
I i ---e	— *marine*,	marie—quiet.
O o ---o	— *over*,	ono—sweet.
U u ---oo	—*rule*,	nui—large.

CONSONANTS.	*Names.*	CONSONANTS.	*Names.*
B b	be	**N n**	nu
D d	de	**P p**	pi
H h	he	**R r**	ro
K k	ke	**T t**	ti
L l	la	**V v**	vi
M m	mu	**W w**	we

The following are used in spelling foreign words:

| **F f** | fe | **S s** | se |
| **G g** | ge | **Y y** | yi |

He pu-u.

first of these was the sound that separates the two vowels in the word below, which means 'hill'.

The Glottal Stop

This sound is made in much the same way as a *p* or a *k*, but instead of the lips or tongue producing it, the vocal cords do so. Because it isn't really a consonant in English, it's hard to give an example of what it sounds like. However, you can hear it between the vowels in the expression *Oh-oh*. In Hawaiian, its status is different, and it is just as much a consonant as *p*, *k*, *l*, *m*, or any of the others.

However, probably because there was no conventional way to write the sound, and because it seemed so different from English consonants, the glottal stop was seldom written. And in the nineteenth century, when most readers of Hawaiian already knew the language, leaving it out seldom caused any difficulties, since context would usually tell the reader which meaning was intended. For example, the picture below obviously refers to *i'a* 'fish' rather than to *ia* 'he, she, it'.

He ia.

The captions under all the woodblock prints contain the word *he*, which is often translated as 'a' or 'an'. But it can also mean 'It's a _____.' Thus, *he i'a* can mean either 'a fish' or 'it's a fish'.

Even without the illustration, no speaker of Hawaiian would confuse the two words, since they belong to different parts of speech and would never appear in the same parts of a sentence. Thus, it was not considered necessary to mark the glottal stop in such words, since every native speaker knew it was there.

Newcomers to the language could pick up clues as to how some words were pronounced, for double vowels were a fairly reliable sign that a glottal stop was present. For example, the following words:

He wa-a.

He ka-a.

He mo-o.

are actually:

      wa'a   **ka'a**

                  mo'o

With some words, however, it was impossible to tell whether or not a glottal stop was present, for there were no double vowels, and context was useless: for example, *kou* 'your' and *ko‘u* 'my' appear in exactly the same context. Thus, as early as 1823, an apostrophe showed that such words were different, a convention that was used regularly, even for the translation of the Bible. Today the glottal stop is written with a reversed apostrophe (').

Now, over a century and a half later, when many people learn Hawaiian by eye as well as by ear, it is essential to write this sound. Not only is it the only difference between many pairs of words such as the following:

mai	from	*ma‘i*	ill
moa	chicken	*mo‘a*	cooked

but unless it is written, a student of the language has no chance of pronouncing correctly a word that is spelled with a sequence of two or more vowels.

Long Vowels

He pu.

The second unwritten sound was actually a group of sounds: five long vowels. Here, 'long' means that the vowels are drawn out, but the quality is not changed very much. For one-syllable nouns, verbs, and adjectives, such as *pū* 'conch shell' above, ignoring the vowel length was not a problem, since in such words the vowel is always long. But in words of two or more syllables, confusing long and short vowels often led to misunderstandings. The following examples show that lengthening the vowel makes the word completely different, just as much as changing the English word *bit* to *bet*. (The long vowels are marked by a straight line, called a *kahakō* in Hawaiian and a *macron* in English.)

'aina	meal	*'āina*	land
kane	skin disease	*kāne*	male
pa'u	soot	*pa'ū*	moist
mana	power	*māna*	chewed mass
'o'o	to crow	*'ō'ō*	digging stick

The following examples show how some common words were once written:

He o.

He pa.

He ka.

Now these words are written

ō

pā   kā

Although once used only in teaching materials, these extra but essential symbols—both the glottal stop (reversed apostrophe) and the macron (line over the vowels)—are finally becoming more widely used on street signs, on maps, and in publications. For example, as opposed to *Hawaii, Kauai, Kalakaua*, and *Waikiki*, the spellings *Hawai'i, Kaua'i, Kalākaua*, and *Waikīkī* give you a much better chance of pronouncing the names accurately.

But you need a few guidelines. The following list shows what sounds correspond to the letters of the Hawaiian alphabet. First, it is important to remember two things about a guide to pronouncing Hawaiian: (1) Although the English examples are close to the Hawaiian sounds, they do not match them exactly; and (2) The pronunciation of some vowels changes slightly, depending on whether they are accented or unaccented, and what their neighboring sounds are.

How to Pronounce the Vowels

a as in   **fa**ther
e as in   **bai**t (without a glide after the vowel)
i as in   **bee**t (without a glide after the vowel)
o as in   **boa**t (without a glide after the vowel)
u as in   **boo**t (without a glide after the vowel)

Each of these vowels can be pronounced long, with little change in quality from that of the short accented vowels. As shown earlier, long vowels are now marked with macrons —ā ē ī ō ū—and their pronunciation does not change much, no matter what position they are in.

Certain combinations of two vowels are pronounced as diphthongs, with the emphasis on the first vowel and the two sounds making up just one syllable:

ai   ae   au   ao   ei   eu   oi   ou   iu.

The first two pairs are difficult for speakers of English, who tend to confuse *ai* with *ae*, and *au* with *ao*, since English has just one diphthong corresponding to each of the pairs. The easiest way to tell them apart is to listen carefully to the first vowel. When *a* is followed by *e* or *o*, it keeps its usual sound. In the following examples, square brackets show the phonetics, or detailed pronunciation.

mae [mae] 'fade'   *mao* [mao] 'alleviate'

But when *a* is followed by *i* or *u*, it changes to a vowel like that in the English word *come*, which we write phonetically as [ə]. For example, it has this sound in:

mai [məi] 'hither, at'   *mau* [məu] 'steady'

This change may take place even when there is no diphthong, but the *i* or *u* is in the next syllable, with a consonant between the vowels, as in:

pali [pəli] 'precipice' *anu* [ənu] 'cool'

Finally, the vowel may also have this sound in a succession of *a*-syllables:

mana [mənə] power
Ka'a'awa [kə'ə'əvə] (a place name meaning 'the wrasse fish')

A usually changes to the [ə] sound in unaccented syllables as well.

As for the other vowels in unaccented syllables, although *o* seems to change little, *e* becomes more like the vowel in *bet*, *i* like the vowel in *bit*, and *u* like the vowel in *book*.

Sometimes (but not always) even an accented *e* has the 'b**e**t' sound when it is next to an *l* or *n*, as in the words *hele* 'go', *mele* 'song', or *kenikeni* 'ten cents'.

How to Pronounce the Consonants

p as in s**p**in (with little air released)
k as in s**k**in (with little air released)
h as in **h**ouse
m as in **m**at
n as in **n**o
l as in **l**ie
w as in **w**ear / **v**ery
‘ the glottal stop (described above)

There are no hard and fast rules for the pronunciation of *w*, except for a tendency for [w], rather than [v], after *o* or *u*. Otherwise, you simply have to listen to native speakers to hear how individual words are pronounced.

How Accent Works

When you hear Hawaiian spoken, you'll notice that some parts of a word are more prominent than others—that is, they are accented. In shorter words, accent is predictable, occurring on:

1. the second-to-last vowel (if all vowels are short):
máka eye   *kanáka* person

2. a diphthong (short or long):
láu leaf   *piláu* rotten
'áina meal   *'áina* land

3. or a long vowel:
Ka'ú (place name)
manó shark

These examples, with different combinations of short and long vowels, and short and long diphthongs, represent different ACCENT UNITS, the building blocks that combine to form longer words. In the following examples, these units are separated by periods:

pule.lehua   butterfly   *makua.hine*   mother, aunt

showing that the accents are:

púle.lehúa   *makúa.híne*

with the last accent in the word (or phrase) emphasized slightly. By the way, this pair of words proves that in spite of many statements to the contrary, the first accent in a five-syllable word is not predictable.

Let's see how this system works on longer words. For instance, the name of the highway leading to Hanauma Bay and beyond (named after a Hawaiian prince and congressional delegate) is rather formidable when seen as a whole word:

KALANIANA'OLE

However, with the accent units marked, it is much more manageable:

KALANI.ANA.'OLE

This marking shows that there's an accent on the second-to-the-last syllable in each unit. If we wrote these accents on the vowels, the word would look like this:

KALÁNI.ÁNA.'ÓLE

But since the accent units themselves are shown, the accent marks aren't necessary.

One extreme example (a word well known because it's used in the last line of a perennially popular song) is the word for 'triggerfish':

HUMUHUMUNUKUNUKUĀPUAʻA

Try to pronounce that! But if it's written this way:

HUMU.HUMU.NUKU.NUKU.Ā.PUAʻA

you have a much better chance of pronouncing it. Each unit is accented as if it were a separate word, and, as noted earlier, the last accent is slightly stronger than the others.

To help readers pronounce longer words, the more recent editions of the *Hawaiian Dictionary* show the accent units for each entry. And from this point on, we'll mark them in the same way. Just remember—the periods aren't part of the spelling system but are shown only to help you pronounce the words accurately.

Grammar

One feature of Hawaiian that prompted early observers to call it childlike is that it often repeats one or two syllables of a word to modify the meaning. The new form usually refers to actions that are repeated, frequent, or done by many people. This feature, which is anything but childlike, and is found in all the other Polynesian languages as well, enriches the vocabulary and expresses subtle distinctions that another language might manage only by adding phrases or coining new words. Examples are:

kuʻi	to punch	*kuʻi.kuʻi*	to box—that is, to punch repeatedly
ʻau	swim	*ʻau.ʻau*	bathe
haʻi	say	*haʻi.haʻi*	speak back and forth
maʻi	sick	*maʻi.maʻi*	chronically sick
hoe	paddle	*hoe.hoe*	paddle continuously

Using the prefix *hoʻo* is another way Hawaiian can modify a word. Although *hoʻo* has a number of meanings, the most common is CAUSATIVE. For example:

nani	pretty	***ho'o.nani***	to beautify
nui	large	***ho'o.nui***	to enlarge
ma'e.ma'e	clean	***ho'o.ma'e.ma'e***	to clean
pono	correct	***ho'o.pono***	to behave correctly
hui	club	***ho'o.hui***	to form a club
hano.hano	honorable	***ho'o.hano.hano***	to honor
luhi	tired	***ho'o.luhi***	to overburden

However, Hawaiian does most of its grammatical work with short words, or markers, that cluster around the main word. For example, rather than adding a suffix (as English does) to form a plural, Hawaiian places a marker in front of the word. The following pair shows one possibility:

wa'a   canoe   *nā wa'a*   canoes

Several other words, such as *mau, pu'u,* or *po'e,* can also form a plural.

Hawaiian verbs are even more different from English. Instead of emphasizing *when* something was done, Hawaiian seems to attach more importance to whether or not an action has begun or is finished. Thus, verbs are marked not for tense, but for a feature called ASPECT, which highlights something other than absolute time. For example, the aspect marker *ua* can emphasize a distinction such as:

Ola ke keiki.   The child is well.
Ua ola ke keiki. The child has become well (but was ill before).

Ua can also indicate that an action has been completed, as in:

Ua *hele au.*   I went.

Two other markers, which surround the verb, can do just the opposite, emphasizing that a state or action is not yet complete:

E *hele* **ana** *au.*   I am going/will go.

These markers can be used for the past and future as well; they simply show that the action hasn't been finished. When used for the future, they show that the action hasn't even begun.

Some parts of the language are far more detailed than in English or Latin. For example, the pronouns indicate not only singular and plural, but DUAL as well—that is, referring to two persons. For example:

'oe	you (1)	*ia*	he, she, it (Hawaiian doesn't distinguish among feminine, masculine, and neuter)
'olua	you (2)	*lāua*	they (2)
'ou.kou	you (plural)	*lā.kou*	they (plural)

Moreover, when a speaker of Hawaiian says the equivalent of 'we', you (the hearer) know whether or not you are included.

kāua	you and I
māua	someone else and I
kā.kou	you, one or more other people, and I
mā.kou	two or more other people and I

Hawaiian also has two ways of saying 'my' (or any of the other possessives), depending on the kind of relationship between the possessor and the possessed. In one type, called INALIENABLE, the possessor has no control over the relationship, in the sense that he or she can neither begin it nor end it. Inalienable relationships (marked within the possessive word by *o*) often involve body parts, innate qualities, parts of a whole, and kin at your own level (brother, sister, etc.) or above (parents, grandparents, etc.):

ko'u lima	my hand
ko'u kupuna	my grandparent
ko'u maka	my eye
ko'u hoa.hā.nau	my cousin
ko'u makua.kāne	my father
kona loko	its interior

Other than a few items of cultural importance (such as land, house, or canoe) or those that you have a spatial relationship with or close connection to (such as boats, vehicles, houses, or clothing), the relationship one has with most objects is ALIENABLE. Children, spouse, and grandchildren are also alienable, all marked by *a* or *ā*:

ka'u puke	my book	*ka'u kumu*	my teacher

ka'u keiki	my child	*ka'u kalo*	my taro
kāna wahine	his wife	*kāna ipo*	her sweetheart

A third way of expressing the idea of 'my', one that uses neither *o* nor *a* is *ku'u*, which often implies affection:

ku'u ipo	my sweetheart
ku'u lei	my child (*lei* 'garland' is used metaphorically here)

Unlike gender systems in such languages as German or French, Hawaiian words don't *belong* to one class or another. Instead, it is the relationship between the possessor and the object or person possessed that conditions the choice of *a* or *o*. When this relationship changes, the possessive marker also changes. Note the following pairs:

ka'u ki'i	my picture (that I own)
ko'u ki'i	my picture (of me)
ka'u lei	my lei (that I made)
ko'u lei	my lei (given to me)

Word Order

The usual order of phrases in a Hawaiian sentence is the reverse of that in English. In other words, the predicate comes first, and is followed by the subject:

[*Ke hula nei*]   [*ka wahine*]
Lit., [Is dancing the hula] [the woman]

Following the same pattern, adjectives follow the nouns they modify:

> *He hale ia.*   It's a house.
> *He hale nui ia.*   It's a big house.

These last two phrases show one of the ways Hawaiian handles sentences in which English uses *be*, for which there is no direct translation. Here, the marker *he* IDENTIFIES something as a house. It can also indicate qualities:

> *He mai.ka'i*   It's good.

(Incidentally, this phrase was the first example of the Hawaiian language in Captain Cook's journal, recording the reaction of Hawaiians to the iron they saw aboard ship.)

To equate two ideas—such as in the English 'She's the teacher', Hawaiian puts the two phrases together, marking the first with *'o*:

> [*'O ke kumu*]   [*ia*]
> Lit., [Is the teacher]   [she]

Hawaiian, like some other Oceanic languages, also lacks a direct translation for *have*. Instead, it uses various possessive constructions to express this idea:

> *He hale ko lāua*   They (2) have a house
> *He pō.poki kā Pua*   Pua has a cat

Variations on a Theme

The sentences you've seen so far are fairly simple. Naturally, Hawaiian has ways of elaborating on them to give more information and fill in the details. For example, it has a closed list of nine nouns that indicate location:

luna	above	*lalo*	below
loko	inside	*waho*	outside
kai	seaward	*uka*	landward, interior
mua	ahead	*waena*	middle
hope	behind		

These words combine with the markers *i* and *ma* to form prepositional phrases that show where something or someone is located, or where it's headed. For example,

i mua	forward
ma loko o ka hale	inside the house
ma waho o ka hale	outside the house

(Many speakers of English in Hawai'i use the expressions *ma kai* 'toward the sea' and *ma uka* 'toward the mountains or interior', rather than absolute compass directions.)

Other markers show directions:

mai	toward speaker or focus	*aku*	away from speaker or focus
a'e	up	*iho*	down

For example:

> *Hele mai!*   Come here!
> *Hele aku!*   Go away!

Such grammatical markers (perhaps as many as 160 in all!) provide the glue that binds these refinements to the basic sentence. In addition to showing location or direction, some others emphasize the word they follow:

> *Maui **nō** ka ʻoi!*   Maui's the best!
> *Au   **nō** hoʻi*   What a terrible thing!

To show how some of these markers work, let's begin with a very simple sentence:

> [*Noho au*]   I sit/sat.
> sit I

(Note, again, that the word order is the opposite of that in English.)
Next, we can add a location phrase:

> [*Noho au*] [*ma luna*]   I sat on top.

and finally a possessive phrase that makes *luna* more specific:

> [*Noho au*] [*ma luna*] [*o ka pō.haku*]
> I sat on top of the rock.

Time phrases add detail as well:

[*I nehi.nei*] [*noho au*] [*ma luna*] [*o ka pō.haku*]
Yesterday I sat on top of the rock.

as do demonstratives:

[*I nehi.nei*] [*noho au*] [*ma luna*][*o kēnā pō.haku*]
Yesterday I sat on top of that rock (by you).

With this last addition, we see another way in which Hawaiian divides the world into finer pieces than does English. Rather than indicating just *this* and *that*, Hawaiian makes a three-way distinction:

kē ia	this (by me)
kē.nā	that (by you)
kē.lā	that (by neither me nor you)

How to Ask Questions

Like many of the world's languages, Hawaiian has two ways of asking questions. The first is to use a word that, in a sense, has a question built into it:

aha	what	*wai*	who
hea	where	*hia*	how many

Because these words work just like nouns or other content words, they are not markers, but appear *with* markers. For example:

He aha kēia?	What's this?
ʻO wai kou inoa?	What's your name?
Ma hea?	Where?
ʻE hia?	How many?

The second way to ask questions is simply to use the word order for a statement, but to change the intonation. With a statement, the pattern is roughly this:

Here, the sentence means 'This is a book.' But with this pattern:

it means 'Is this a book?' This is how to ask a question that would be answered with 'yes' (*ʻae*) or 'no' (*ʻaʻole / ʻaʻale*).

This second way of asking questions is probably the source for a similar pattern in local English, which many new residents pick up unconsciously in a surprisingly short time.

Of course, this short sketch only skims the surface of Hawaiian grammar. For more detail, see *Ka Lei Haʻaheo* and *The Hawaiian Sentence Book*.

Vocabulary

Many early critics of the Hawaiian vocabulary were concerned mainly with its size (some thought it too large; others, too small) and what they thought was a lack of generic terms. However, the people who made such complaints probably did so because they expected all languages to look at the world in the same way that English does.

Hawaiian Vocabulary as a Reflection of Culture

It has long been noted that Hawaiian is especially rich in words in areas that were or are of particular importance to the speakers of the language. For example, compilers of dictionaries have found a great many terms for taro and sweet potato, and for winds, clouds, and rains. Other categories well represented in the vocabulary are fish, birds, canoes, *kapa* (bark cloth), amusements and games, kin terms, tools, weapons, and deities connected with the indigenous religion—among many others.

Bible translators found the mismatch between the Hawaiian and English vocabularies to be a practical problem, as was the difference between literal and figurative meanings of words. Certainly such differences are common in many languages; indeed, what happens below the surface meanings of words is important for any appreciation of language as an art form, particularly poetry. But in Hawaiian, figurative meaning (called *kaona*) was much more common than in English. Sometimes the *kaona* was obvious, but at other times, it was so obscure that only a few people knew it. From a poetic point of view, Hawaiians considered the hidden meaning more important than the one on the surface. Today, however, because of the limited use of the language, much of the *kaona* of the old legends and chants has been forgotten.

English Words in Hawaiian

He ki. **He ka-o.**

An even greater problem for the translators, and for the Hawaiians themselves, was that there were no words available for the new objects and ideas that were introduced from the European and American cultures. At first, new words trickled into the language, but the missionaries, who concentrated on Bible translation, opened the floodgates for borrowings.

It was not as though Hawaiian could not form new words on its own. Earlier, you saw two ways of doing that, and there are certainly many more. But whenever two languages are in contact for more than a brief time, borrowing almost always takes place.

The first evidence we have for true borrowings comes as early as 1791, when a Spanish ship captain wrote *tropi* for 'rope', most likely from *ta ropi*, with *ta* (now *ka* in most parts of Hawai'i) as the definite article. Another was *tenu* (probably *tenū*) for 'canoe'.

Twenty years later, many more words were entering the language. On an 1810 list of about 400 words, we find 41 that refer to recent additions to the Hawaiian culture. Not all these are borrowings, for some were simply Hawaiian words that had been modified for the new meanings. But the following words are true borrowings, and they include both common nouns and names of people and countries:

lummee	rum	*Itseeke*	Isaac
tabete	cabbage	*Keone*	John
Keeme	James	*Pritane*	England
Williama	William	*Merikana*	American

As for the actual letters used in the new words, note that several consonants appear that are no longer part of the Hawaiian alphabet—*b*, *r*, *s*, and *t*. This is because the early explorers and beachcombers had no guidelines to follow except the spelling patterns of their native language. After 1826, when the official Hawaiian alphabet was adopted, those words were changed as follows:

lama	rum	*Ika.'aka*	Isaac
kā.piki	cabbage	*Keoni*	John
Kimo	James	*Pele.kania*	Britain
Wili.ama	William	*'Ame.lika*	America

The most striking difference between the English and Hawaiian forms is due to a feature mentioned earlier: Hawaiian has no consonant clusters, and no word can end in a consonant. Thus, a vowel is added or inserted where necessary. A classic example is the word for 'Christmas': *Kaliki.maka*. The following diagram shows the relationship between the English and the Hawaiian sounds. Note the vowels that have been added:

$$k \quad r \quad \textup{I} \quad s \quad m \quad \textschwa \quad s$$
$$ka \quad l \quad i \quad ki \quad m \quad a \quad ka$$

with the result that a two-syllable English word becomes a five-syllable Hawaiian word. The following examples show one-syllable words in English (*pin, beef, horse*—reinterpreted to mean *mule*, and *sheep*) that have become two-syllable Hawaiian words.

He pi-ne.

He pi-pi.

He ho-ki.

He hi-pa.

In some words, a consonant cluster has been simplified by dropping one of the sounds, especially if the two sounds are made at the same position. For example, in the following words:

'ai.lana island   *kaila* style

nd and *st* have not been split up, but instead, simplified.

Another important difference is due simply to the relative smallness of the Hawaiian alphabet: It has only eight consonants, while English has twenty-four. If Hawaiian has sounds that are close to the English ones, the borrowed words are fairly recognizable:

maine	mine	*malina*	marine
moni	money	*numo.nia*	pneumonia

Many Hawaiian borrowings, however, do not sound much like the English words on which they were based. For example, Hawaiian *k* has to substitute for eleven different English consonants, the sounds printed in boldface in the following words:

time	**s**ee	**ch**urch
dime	**z**oo	**k**eep
thigh	mea**s**ure	**g**o
then	**j**udge	

Take, for example, the word *kī*. In addition to several indigenous meanings, it is also the borrowed form for the English words *key*, *tea*, and *Gee*!

Hawaiian Words in English

When two languages are in contact, borrowing is seldom a one-way street. Polynesian words have been used in English for over two centuries, but we're not usually aware of them. Two words in particular are *taboo*, from Tongan *tapu*, and *tattoo*, from Tahitian *tātau*. (The Hawaiian versions are *kapu* and *kā.kau*.)

Usually, words are borrowed when there is a need for them. From the English-language point of view, the most obvious need for Hawaiian words has been to name plants, animals, marine life, and activities and objects that exist only in the Hawaiian culture. The following are just a few examples of words that may not be used in general English, but still have made their way into unabridged dictionaries:

Fish

'ahi	yellowfin tuna	*aku*	bonito
akule	big-eyed scad	*walu*	oilfish

Birds

'ele.paio	flycatcher	*nē.nē*	Hawaiian goose
'i'iwi	scarlet honeycreeper		

Plants

nau.paka	a kind of shrub	*limu*	seaweed, moss
hau	hibiscus tiliaceus	*hala*	pandanus

Geological features

'a'ā and *pā.hoe.hoe*   types of lava

Culture

hā.nai	adopted	*mana*	power
heiau	terrace or platform for worship		
kā.hili	feather standard	*kahuna*	priest, expert
'au.makua	personal god		
maka.hiki	seasonal celebration		

Words and Phrases a Visitor Is Likely to Hear

He ha-le.

He la.

Even though the borrowings above have been certified, as it were, by being entered in English unabridged dictionaries, they are mostly words for specialists. But the everyday English spoken in the Islands is liberally sprinkled with other Hawaiian words and phrases. The commonest of these are place names.

Place Names

Everyone in Hawai'i talks about places, and most of their names have a Hawaiian origin. Although some are so old that their meaning is unclear, the place names that people use today can be usually be explained. Sometimes a name

He pu·u.

commemorates a Hawaiian mythological hero, such as *Pele*, a Honolulu street named after the volcano goddess, Pele. But often, a feature of the landscape figures in the name. The following list shows a few of the most common words used:

'āina	land	*moana*	sea
ala	way, path	*moku*	island
ana	cave	*olo*	hill
ao	cloud	*one*	sand
awa	port, harbor	*niu*	coconut
hale	house	*pā*	enclosure
hana/hono	bay	*pali*	precipice, cliff
honua	land	*papa*	plain
'ili.'ili	pebbles	*pō.haku*	rock
kai	sea	*po'o*	head
kahua	site	*pua*	flower
Kāne	the god Kāne	*pua'a*	pig
kua	ridge	*puka*	hole
kukui	candlenut tree	*puna*	spring
kula	plain, upland	*pu'u*	hill
lae	point	*wa'a*	canoe
lua	pit, two	*wai*	water
mauna	mountain		

Many place names are a combination of these words, such as *Ala Wai* 'waterway', *Ala Moana* 'seaway', or *Mauna Lani* 'heavenly mountain'. But more often, these words are qualified by a following adjective. For example:

'ele.'ele	black	*kea*	white
hou	new	*lani*	heavenly
iki	small	*loa*	long, big
kapu	forbidden	*mea*	red
nani	pretty	*nui*	large
kahiko	ancient	*uka*	interior
kai	sea	*'ula*	red

Thus, *Mauna Kea* 'white mountain', *Mauna Loa* 'long mountain', *Puna.hou* 'new spring', *Wai.loa* 'long water', *Pu'u.loa* 'long hill'. It's important to remember, however, that these words *follow* the word they qualify. Some place names are backwards, having been formed according to English, rather than Hawaiian, structure. For example, if *Lani.kai* was meant to translate 'heavenly sea', it should have been *Kai.lani*.

Commonly Mispronounced Place Names

Perhaps place names provide you the best chance to pronounce Hawaiian words. You should try to be as accurate as possible. The following list shows the most common mistakes speakers of English (even longtime residents) make when pronouncing Hawaiian:

1. Often the glottal stop is left out. For example, *Kauai* (*cow-eye!*) instead of *Kau.a'i*.

2. Next, long vowels are ignored unless the expected accent pattern is changed (however, the common mispronunciation of *Kū.hiō* as *Kuhío* is a mystery; see the following list). We seem to reproduce the long vowel in the last syllable of *Wai.kī.kī* because its accent is unexpected, but we usually miss the preceding one.

3. Unaccented vowels are often changed to *uh* [ə]. This change is normal for *a*, but not for the other vowels. For example, *Mólə.kai* instead of *Molo.kaʻi*.

4. Unaccented vowels are also sometimes dropped altogether: *Kiə.moku* instead of *Keʻe.au.moku*.

5. *H* tends to be dropped in an unaccented syllable: *Kəmea.mea* instead of *Kameha.meha*.

6. Final unaccented *-e* is pronounced like *-i*, following the English pattern: *Lihui* instead of *Lī.huʻe*.

7. Words spelled with *a* tend to be pronounced with the

vowel in the word *cat*, a sound that definitely does not exist in Hawaiian. The first vowel in the street name *Kapiʻo.lani* is often pronounced with this vowel.

A logical place to begin is with the names of the islands. Of the major islands, Maui is the only one without a glottal stop in the name. From north to south, the islands are:

Kau.aʻi	not *Káuai*
Niʻi.hau	not *Nī.hau*
Oʻahu	not *Owahu*
Molo.kaʻi	not *Mólə.kai*
Maui	
Lā.naʻi	not *Lənai*
Kahoʻo.lawe	not *Káho.lawe*
Hawaiʻi	not *Hawai* or *Hawaia* (You must listen and decide for yourself whether a *w*-like or a *v*-like sound is used in this word.)

The following list shows area names on Oʻahu that are often mispronounced:

Any name with *ʻĀina*	*Mā.noa*
ʻĀ.lewa	*Mō.ʻili.ʻili*
Haʻ.ikū	*Nā.nā.kuli*
Hā.lawa	*Pā.lama*
Hale.ʻiwa	*Pā.lolo*
Kalā.heo	*Pō.kaʻī*
Kāne.ʻohe	*Puna.luʻu*
Kapā.lama	*Wahi.awā*

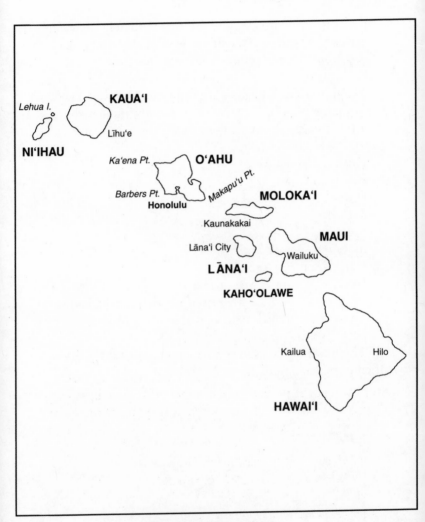

The Hawaiian Islands

Lā.ʻie	*Wai.ʻalae*
Mā.ʻili	*Wai.kī.kī*
Mā.kaha	*Wai.piʻo*

The following street names in Honolulu are often mispronounced:

ʻEna	not *ʻIna*
Kaʻiu.lani	not *Kaiə.lani*
Kalā.kaua	not *Kalə.kawa*
Kalani.ana.ʻole	not *Kalani.ana.oli*
Kapiʻo.lani	not *Cápiə.lani*
Keʻe.au.moku	not *Kiə.moku*
Kī.lau.ea	not *Kilə.wea*
Kū.hiō	not *Kuhío*
Liliʻu.oka.lani	not Lilly.kəlani

Everyday Words

Even when Hawaiʻi residents aren't talking about places, they use many Hawaiian words and phrases, sometimes forgetting that not everyone knows what they mean. Here are some you are likely to hear:

A hui hou.	Good-bye.
A hui hou aku.	Good-bye (response).
ʻĀ.ʻoia.	That's it.
E kala mai iaʻu.	Pardon me.
E ʻolu.ʻolu ʻoe.	Please.

'Ewa	west, toward 'Ewa town
hana	work
Hana hou	Do it again.
hila.hila	embarrassed
ho'o.mali.mali	excessive flattery (less common now than earlier)
ho'o.pono.pono	family conferences for settling disputes
huki.lau	pull-net fishing
hula	dance with chant
kama.'āina	native
kāne	man, male
koa	type of hardwood
kō.kua	help
kolohe	naughty
kukui	candlenut
kule.ana	territory, privilege, responsibility
lā.nai	porch, terrace
lei	garland
lua	toilet
lū.'au	feast
Mahalo.	Thank you.
mai.ka'i	good, well
ma kai	toward the sea
mali.hini	newcomer
ma uka	toward the mountains
mele	song
mu'u.mu'u	full-length dress
'ohana	family
'ono	delicious
pau	finished

pau hana	quitting time
Pehea 'oe?	How are you?
pili.kia	trouble
pono	right, proper
puka	hole (perforation)
pū.pule	crazy
wahine	woman, female

Menu Hawaiian

He mo-a.

Another place you're likely to find Hawaiian words is on a menu, since many restaurants serve a sampling of Hawaiian dishes. Here are some of the food terms you might find.

Appetizers

pū.pū   once referring to the food served with *'awa* (a traditional drink), the word is now used for hors d'oeuvre.

lomi.lomi salmon   salt salmon, now minced but original-
   ly   hand shredded (*lomi.lomi* 'massage'), with onion
   and tomato.
poke   cubed, marinated, and spiced raw fish or other
   seafood (*poke* 'sliced, cut')
limu   edible seaweed

Main course

huli.huli   barbequed or cooked on a spit, e.g., chicken.
   Moa hoʻohulihuli means chicken cooked in this way
   (*huli* 'turn')
iʻa   fish. Some common types:
   aku   skipjack
   aʻu   swordfish
   mahi.mahi   dolphin fish (*not* a dolphin!)
   ʻō.pelu   mackeral skad
   walu   oilfish
puaʻa   pig
kā.lua pig, chicken, or turkey   meat or fowl baked in an
   imu 'earth oven' (*kā.lua* 'cause-pit')
lau.lau   *kālua* pork (or chicken) and butterfish wrapped
   in *kalo* 'taro' leaves and baked
mana.pua   Chinese pork cake (from *mea ʻono puaʻa*
   'delicious pig thing')
moa   chicken
moa me ka laiki loloa   chicken (with) long-rice
pipi   beef (Eng.)
pipi kaula   jerked beef
ʻō.pū pipi   tripe stew

He la-u.   **He pu-a-a.**

Starch

kalo taro   *uhi* yam
poi taro paste   *laiki* rice (Eng.)
'uala sweet potato

Dessert

hau.pia cold *pia* 'arrowroot' or cornstarch and
    coconut cream pudding
kū.lolo cooked *kalo* 'taro' and coconut cream pudding

Drinks

mai.tai *lama* (rum) and fruitjuice
'okole.hau distilled *kī* 'ti' root spirits
pia beer (Eng.)
waina wine (Eng.)

And how do you respond to the *mea.'ai* 'food'? Two very
common expressions are:

'Ono! Delicious!
Mā.'ana / Mā.'ona! Fully satisfied!

Vocabulary in Hawaiian Lyrics

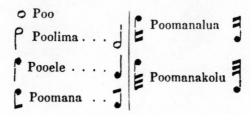

After dinner, it's time for Hawaiian music. Whether the lyrics are entirely in Hawaiian, or a mixture of Hawaiian and English (*hapa haole*), it's almost certain that the songs you hear will use some of the following words.

'a'ala	fragrant
ahi.ahi	evening
akua	god
aloha	love
ā.nue.nue	rainbow
au	I
Au.ē!	Alas!
'awa.puhi	ginger
ha'a.heo	proud
Ha'ina mai *ka puana*	Tell the summary refrain (of a song).
hala	pandanus
hano.hano	honored
hau	dew
hemo.lele	glorious

hoa pili	close friend
hoʻi mai	return
honi	kiss
ʻi.lima	Oʻahu's flower
inoa	name
ipo	sweetheart
kahiko	olden, ancient
kali	wait
kani	to sound
kila.kila	majestic
kō.nane	bright
kuʻu home	
(Eng.)	my home
lā.hui	race, nation
lani	heavenly, royal
lehua	*lehua* blossom
lei	garland
lele	to fly
leo	voice
lewa	sky
lima	hand
loke, rose	
(Eng.)	rose
maha	repose
mahina	moon
maile	vine for a traditional *lei*
maka	eye, face
makani	wind
make.make	want
makua	parent

mā.lama	care for
mā.lie	calm
malu	shade
mana‘o	thought
manawa	time
manu	bird
mau	constant
mea	thing
mele	song
mili.mili	beloved
mō.‘ī	sovereign
moki.hana	Kaua‘i's *lei*
nahe.nahe	gentle, sweet, soft
nani	pretty
noe	mist
noho	stay, sit, dwell
‘oe	thou
ola	life, live
‘ole	without
‘olu.‘olu	cool, comfortable
ona.ona	fragrant, gentle
pane	answer
pī.kake (Eng., from *peacock*)	jasmine
pili	cling
pō	night
poina	forget
poina ‘ole	unforgettable
pono	right
pua	flower, child

pume.hana	warm, affectionate
puʻu.wai	heart
sila (Eng.)	seal
ua	rain
uʻi	beautiful
wai	water
waiho	leave
wai.lele	waterfall
wale nō	only

Hotel Names

Many hotels may also have Hawaiian names, which often refer to the area where the hotel is located: *Mauna Kea, Mauna Loa, Poʻi.pū, Wai.kī.kī.* The Hawaiian word may be combined with an English word that conjures up island life or Hawaiian royalty: *Banyan, Beach, Breakers, Coconut, King, Ocean, Palm, Prince, Princess, Queen, Reef, Sands, Shores.* The following Hawaiian words are also common in hotel names:

ala	way
aliʻi	chief
aloha	aloha
huki.lau	pull-net fishing
ʻili.kai	surface of the sea
ʻi.lima	Oʻahu's flower
kai	sea
kau.lana	famous
koa	hardwood tree (Hawaiian "mahogany")

THE HAWAIIAN HOTEL!

THE PROPRIETOR WILL SPARE NO
pains to make this

ELEGANT HOTEL

First-Class in Every Particular!

ROOMS CAN BE HAD BY THE NIGHT OR WEEK!

with or without board.

HALL AND LARGE ROOMS TO LET FOR
ju28*   PUBLIC MEETINGS, OR SOCIETIES.   1y

(From *The Honolulu Advertiser,* ca. 1872)

lā.nai	terrace
lani	heavenly
leʻa.leʻa	joyous, sexy
maile	vine for traditional *lei*
mauna	mountain
moana	sea
nani	pretty
pua	flower
wai	water
pū.nā.wai	water spring

The Future of Hawaiian

Late in the nineteenth century and through the first half of the twentieth, a number of developments (competition from English, reduction in the Hawaiian population, annexation by the United States, and policy decisions by the Department of Education) resulted in a drastic drop in the number of native Hawaiian speakers. Some estimate the figure today to be as low as one thousand—and many of those are elderly. In the last two decades, however, a renaissance in language and culture has stopped, or at least slowed down, Hawaiian's slide toward extinction.

One of the most important outgrowths of the renaissance is *Nā Pū.nana Leo* (language nests). Based on an idea from the Māori community in New Zealand, this is a total-immersion program that enables children between the ages of three and five to hear and speak only Hawaiian for ten hours a day, five days a week. In the fall of 1992, there were 131 children enrolled in *Pūnana Leo* schools in the Islands.

After entering the school system, these children have a chance to maintain and improve their skills in Hawaiian in related programs at the elementary and high school levels. And at the university level, enrollment in Hawaiian language classes has risen dramatically since a low point in the early 1960s—so much, in fact, that one often has the pleasure of hearing Hawaiian spoken on the University of Hawai'i campuses.

But no language survives in a vacuum. The Hawaiian renaissance has breathed new life into not only the language, but the culture as well. And in recent years, one of the most prominent cultural changes has been an increased interest in traditional hula—especially through instruction and performances of *nā hā.lau* (hula schools). Thus, *nā hālau*, along with language programs for every age group, provide opportunities for people to gather and speak Hawaiian, giving the language a chance to change, grow, and continue as a living entity.

English-Hawaiian Word List

above, *luna*
adopted, *hānai*
affectionate, *pumehana*
again (do it), *hana hou*
ahead, *mua*
alas, *auē*
alleviate, *mao*
ancient, *kahiko*
answer, *pane*
arrowroot pudding, *haupia*
at, *mai*
aunt, *makuahine*
away, *aku*

baked pork (or chicken), fish,
    taro leaves *laulau*
barbequed, *hulihuli*
bark cloth, *kapa*
bathe, *'au'au*
bay, *hana, hono*
beautiful, *u'i*
beautify, *ho'onani*
beef, *pipi*
beer, *pia*
behave correctly, *ho'opono*
behind, *hope*

beloved, *milimili*
below, *lalo*
best, *'oi*
big, *loa*
big, *nui*
big-eyed scad, *akule*
bird, *manu*
black, *'ele'ele*
bonito, *aku*
book, *puke*
box, to, *ku'iku'i*
bright, *kōnane*
butterfly, *pulelehua*

cabbage, *kāpiki*
calm, *mālie*
candlenut, *kukui*
canoe, *wa'a*
canoe bailer, *kā*
care for, *mālama*
cart, *ka'a*
cat, *pōpoki*
causative, *ho'o-*
cave, *ana*
chant with dance, *hula*
chewed mass, *māna*

chicken, *moa*
chicken long rice,
   moa me ka laiki loa
chief, *ali'i*
child, *keiki, lei, pua,*
   kamali'i (pl.)
child of the land, *kama'āina*
Christmas, *Kalikimaka*
clean, *ma'ema'e*
clean, (to), *ho'oma'ema'e*
cliff, *pali*
cling, *pili*
cloud, *ao*
club, *hui*
club, to form, *ho'ohui*
coconut, *niu*
comfortable, *'olu'olu*
conch shell, *pū*
conference to rectify,
   ho'oponpono
constant, *mau*
container, *kā*
converse, *ha'iha'i*
cooked, *mo'a*
cool, *anu, 'olu'olu*
correct, *pono*
cousin, *hoahānau*
crazy, *pūpule*
crow, to, *'o'ō*

dance with chant, *hula*
delicious, *'ono*
dew, *hau*

digging stick, *'ō'ō*
dish, *pā*
dolphin fish, *mahimahi*
down, *iho*
dress (full-length), *mu'umu'u*
drink, *inu*
drum, *pahu*
dwell, *noho*

earth oven, *imu*
eight, *walu, 'ewalu*
embarrassed, *hilahila*
enclosure, *pā*
enlarge, *ho'onui*
evening, *ahiahi*
expert, *kahuna*
eye, *maka*

face, *maka*
fade, *mae*
family, *'ohana*
famous, *kaulana*
father, *makuakāne*
feast, *lū'au*
feather standard, *kāhili*
female, *wahine*
finished, *pau*
fish, *i'a*
fishing (pull-net), *hukilau*
five, *lima, 'elima*
flattery, *ho'omalimali*
flower, *pua*
fly, (to), *lele*

flycatcher, *'elepaio*
food, *mea'ai*
forbidden, *kapu*
forget, *poina*
fork, *'ō*
four, *hā*, *'ehā*
fragrant, *'a'ala*, *onaona*
friend, *hoa pili*
from, *mai*

garland, *lei*
gee, *kī*
gentle, *nahenahe*, *onaona*
ginger, *'awapuhi*
glorious, *hemolele*
go, *hele*
goat, *kao*
god, *akua*
good, *maika'i*
good-bye, *a hui hou (aku)*
goose, *nēnē*
grandparent, *kupuna*

hand, *lima*
harbor, *awa*
Hawaiian-European mix,
    hapa haole
he, *ia*
head, *po'o*
heart, *pu'uwai*
heavenly, *lani*
hello, *aloha*

help, *kōkua*
here, *mai*
hibiscus tiliaceus, *hau*
hidden meaning, *kaona*
hill, *olo*, *pu'u*
his, *kāna*, *kona*
hither, *mai*
hole, *puka*
home, *home*
honor, (to), *ho'ohanohano*
honorable, *hanohano*
hors d'oeuvre, *pūpū*
house, *hale*
how are you?, *pehea 'oe*
how many?, *hia*
hula school, *hālau*

I, *au*
ill, *ma'i*
(incomplete), *e...ana*
indeed, *ho'i ē*, *nō*
ink bottle, *ipu 'īnika*
inside, *loko*
interior, *uka*
island, *'ailana*, *moku*
it, *ia*
its, *kāna*, *kona*

jasmine, *pīkake*
jerked beef, *pipi kaula*
joyous, *le'ale'a*

Kaua'i's lei, *mokihana*
key, *kī*
kiss, *honi*
land, *'āina, honua*
landward, *uka*
large, *nui, loa*
lava (types), *'a'ā, pāhoehoe*
leaf, *lau*
leave, *waiho*
life, *ola*
live, *ola*
lizard, *mo'o*
long, *loa*
long rice, *laiki loloa*
love, *aloha*

mackeral skad, *'ōpelu*
macron, *kahakō*
"mahogany" (Hawaiian), *koa*
majestic, *kilakila*
male, *kāne*
man, *kāne*
marine, *malina*
massage, *lomilomi*
meal, *'aina*
middle, *waena*
mine, *maine*
mist, *noe*
moist, *pa'ū*
money, *moni*
moon, *malama, mahina*
moss, *limu*
mother, *makuahine*

mountain, *mauna*
mule, *hoki*
my, *ko'u, ka'u, ku'u*
name, *inoa*
nation, *lāhui*
native, *kama'āina*
naughty, *kolohe*
nest, *pūnana*
new, *hou*
newcomer, *malihini*
night, *pō*
nine, *iwa, 'eiwa*
no, *'a'ole, 'a'ohe, 'a'ale*
nose, *ihu*

O'ahu's flower, *'īlima*
of, *a, o*
oilfish, *walu*
one, *kahi, 'ekahi, ho'okahi*
only, *wale nō*
outside, *waho*
overburden, *ho'oluhi*

paddle, *hoe*
paddle continuously, *hoehoe*
pandanus, *hala*
pardon me, *e kala mai ia'u*
parent, *makua*
path, *ala*
pebbles, *'ili'ili*
person, *kanaka*
personal god, *'aumakua*
picture, *ki'i*

pig, *pua'a*
pin, *pine*
pit, *lua*
pit-baked, *kālua*
plain, *kula, papa*
platform for worship, *heiau*
please, *e 'olu'olu 'oe*
(plural), *mau, nā, po'e, pu'u*
pneumonia, *numonia*
point, *lae*
porch, *lānai*
pork cake, *manapua*
port, *awa*
power, *mana*
precipice, *pali*
pretty, *nani*
priest, *kahuna*
privilege, *kuleana*
proper, *pono*
proud, *ha'aheo*
punch, *ku'i*

quick, *wikiwiki*
quitting time, *pau hana*

race, *lāhui*
rain, *ua*
rainbow, *ānuenue*
red, *'ula, mea*
repeat, *hana hou*
repeat refrain,
   ha'ina mai ka puana
repose, *maha*

responsibility, *kuleana*
return, *ho'i mai*
rice, *laiki*
ridge, *kua*
right, *pono*
rock, *pōhaku*
rose, *loke, rose*
rotisseried, *hulihuli*
rotten, *pilau*
royal, *lani*
rum, *lama*
rum, fruitjuice cocktail, *maitai*

salmon (minced),
   lomilomi salmon
sand, *one*
sated, *mā'ana, mā'ona*
say, *ha'i*
scarlet honeycreeper, *'i'iwi*
school, *kula*
sea, *moana, kai*
sea surface, *'ilikai*
seafood (marinated), *poke*
seal, *sila*
seasonal celebration, *makahiki*
seaward, *ma kai*
seaweed, *limu*
seven, *hiku, 'ehiku*
sexy, *le'ale'a*
shade, *malu*
shark, *manō*
she, *ia*

sheep, *hipa*
sick, *ma'i*
sick, chronically, *ma'ima'i*
sit, *noho*
site, *kahua*
six, *ono, 'eono*
skin, *'ili*
skin disease, *kane*
skipjack, *aku*
sky, *lani, lewa*
small, *iki*
soft, *nahenahe*
song, *mele*
soot, *pa'u*
sound, ring, *kani*
sovereign, *mō'ī*
speak back and forth, *ha'iha'i*
spouting water, *waikīkī*
spring, *puna*
stay, *noho*
steady, *mau*
style, *kaila*
sun, *lā*
sweet, *nahenahe*
sweet potato, *'uala*
sweetheart, *ipo*
swim, *'au*
swordfish, *a'u*

taboo, *kapu*
taro, *kalo*
taro paste, *poi*
taro pudding, *kūlolo*

tattoo, *kākau*
tea, *kī*
teacher, *kumu*
ten, *'umi*
ten cents, *kenikeni*
terrace, *lānai*
territory, *kuleana*
thank you, *mahalo*
that (by you), *kēnā*
that (far), *kēlā*
that's it, *'ā'oia*
the, *ka, ke*
they (2), *lāua*
they (plural), *lākou*
thing, *mea*
this, *kēia*
thought, *mana'o*
three, *kolu. 'ekolu*
ti root spirits, *'okolehau*
time, *manawa*
tired, *luhi*
toilet, *lua*
tooth, *niho*
toward, *ma, i*
traditional drink, *'awa*
triggerfish,
    humuhumunukunukuāpua'a
tripe stew, *'ōpū pipi*
trouble, *pilikia*
turn, *huli*
turtle, *honu*
two, *lua, 'elua*

underwater plant, *limu*
unforgettable, *poina 'ole*
up, *a'e*
upland, *kula*

visitor, *malihini*
voice, *leo*

wait, *kali*
want, *makemake*
warm, *pumehana*
water, *wai*
water spring, *pūnāwai*
waterfall, *wailele*
way, *ala*
we (2, exclusive), *māua*
we (2, inclusive), *kāua*
we (pl., exclusive), *mākou*
we (pl., inclusive), *kākou*
welcome, *aloha*

well, *maika'i, ola*
what?, *aha*
where?, *hea*
white, *kea*
who?, *wai*
wife, *wahine*
wind, *makani*
wine, *waina*
without, *'ole*
woman, *wahine*
work, *hana*

yam, *uhi*
yellowfin tuna, *'ahi*
yes, *'ae*
yesterday, *i nehinei*
you (1), *'oe*
you (2), *'olua*
you (pl.), *'oukou*
your (1), *kou*

Handy References

If you'd like to learn more about the Hawaiian language, try the following books:

The Voices of Eden: A History of Hawaiian Language Studies, by Albert J. Schütz. Honolulu: University of Hawai'i Press, 1994.

Hawaiian Dictionary, by Mary Kawena Pukui and Samuel H. Elbert. Honolulu: University of Hawai'i Press, 1986.

New Pocket Hawaiian Dictionary, by Mary Kawena Pukui and Samuel H. Elbert. Honolulu: University of Hawai'i Press, 1992.

Place Names of Hawaii, by Mary Kawena Pukui, Samuel H. Elbert, and Esther T. Mookini. Honolulu: University of Hawai'i Press, 1974.

Pocket Place Names of Hawaii, by Mary Kawena Pukui, Samuel H. Elbert, and Esther T. Mookini. Honolulu: University of Hawai'i Press, 1989.

Hawaiian Street Names, by Rich Budnick and Duke Kalani Wise. Honolulu: Aloha Publishing, 1989.

Nā Mele o Hawai'i Nei: 101 Hawaiian Songs, by Samuel H. Elbert and Noelani Mahoe. Honolulu: University of Hawai'i Press, 1970.

Ka Lei Ha'aheo: Beginning Hawaiian, by Alberta Pualani Hopkins. Honolulu: University of Hawai'i Press, 1992.

Learn Hawaiian at Home, by Kahikāhealani Wight. Honolulu: Bess Press, 1992.

The Hawaiian Sentence Book, by Robert Lokomaika'iokalani Snakenberg. Honolulu: Bess Press, 1988.

Aloha!
(It also means good-bye)

About the Author

Albert J. Schütz received his Ph.D. from Cornell University. He is a professor of linguistics at the University of Hawai'i and the author of several books on Fijian, including a reference grammar of the standard language, and of numerous articles on Pacific linguistic history. His work on Fijian suggested a way of looking at the Hawaiian language from a different perspective, which culminated in the publication of *Voices of Eden: A History of Hawaiian Language Studies*.